The Man Who Tried To Hug Clouds

Jim Bennett

Published by bluechrome publishing 2004

2 4 6 8 10 9 7 5 3 1

Copyright © Jim Bennett 2004

First published in Great Britain in 2004 by
bluechrome publishing
An Imprint of KMS Ltd
PO Box 109,
Portishead, Bristol. BS20 7ZJ

www.bluechrome.co.uk

A CIP catalogue record for this book is available from the
British Library

ISBN   1-904781-31-4

The Man Who Tried To Hug Clouds

Jim Bennett

Contents

The man who tried to hug clouds

I knew a man
who tried to hug clouds
he said he loved to watch them
and feel their spirit

he tried hard to reach them
climbed up mountains
stood arms wide to hug
them as they rolled in
and spent themselves against him
he never could
but it didn't stop him trying

his cloud-love often brought him home
wet, frozen and happy
from a wing-walk afternoon
where stapled to bi-plane wing
he rushed through clouds
wind-choked with arms wide

or sent him
rushing off to Blackpool
to climb the tower
when low cloud was forecast

but most of all
he loved the winter
and the road by the churchyard
it was here
when the chill and the air pressure
were just right
that his cloud-love would appear
it would seep from the cemetery
creep over the wall
fill the space to his knees
then well-up into his waiting arms
but always vanished
before he could close them

I knew a man who tried to hug clouds
he never could
but it didn't stop him trying

Liverpool 1s

Liverpool Is

Liverpool is

Liverpool is
town on Saturday
football and beer
Pierhead and ferries
Dale Street Church street
Sefton park and the rec
it's places and people
accents and buildings

Liverpool is

old and new
the Tate and the Walkers
the Spinners and the La's
Christians and McGough
The Liverpool Scene
and the Dead Good Poets
sarcastic and funny
using words like daggers

Liverpool is

a bevie with your mates
having a laugh
the Albert Dock and Canning Street
the Rope Walk Roads
the good old days
the bad old days
poverty and tears
making do

Liverpool is

cathedrals and religion
mosques and temples
chapels and churches
the red, and the blue
the orange and the green
Goodison and Anfield
universities and shopping
students and the homeless
side by side
shoulder to shoulder
with the Pope
in Hope Street

Liverpool is

living in millions of heads
as the sound of
music in a cellar
but it's more than that
it's love and hate
peace and riot
rubbish in the gutter
council houses and
empty factories

Liverpool is

nan bread and pita bread
chips and Chinese
pizza and bagels
an Indian and McDonalds
it's every colour and tradition
it's white and black
brown and yellow
England and Ireland
Wales and Scotland
Pakistan and Bangladesh
India and China
the West Indies and Hong Kong
Somalia and Cameroon
it's every place
its a kaleidoscope
of mixed living
loving colour

Liverpool is

view from another coast

it was a long trip along motorway
dual carriageway through towns and cities
four hours to bisect the country shore to shore
to find the poetry night at Cumberland Arms

over hills and moor and down through valleys
illuminated by the lights of towns
and the glow of distant cities
past the dark looming mills and the bright
sharp lights of other vehicles
past quarry scars and the ghosts of hills
to be welcomed by the angel of the north
and the streets of Newcastle

then there were the Poetry Vandals
a group of local poets
cracking up the room with a perfect phrase
or a gesture which broke through
the lethargy of the everyday
observed events crammed into shapes
like canopies served to be enjoyed

somewhere in the gloom of travel
before returning home that night
I stood on stage and read my poems
read of Liverpool and home
of dockland and children
the view from another coast
spelling out in words
the tyranny of love
the betrayal of politics
the synergies of life
and how time
wipes it all clean

the secret of being a teacher

this is the secret
of being a teacher
the old man said
then without saying more
he moved his hands
and in a shadow
cast onto the wall
a dog ran silently barking
after a terrified cat
then a field of flowers
blew in a light breeze
in another moment
a city sprang up
skyscrapers
scraped the picture rail
and down in the streets
vehicles and people
moved in imitation life
like the fleeting shadows
that they were
before they disappeared
with a flourish and a wave
as the old man
turned and bowed

now it's your turn he said
he made the audience
shape their hands and move them
and in the right light
it looked like
a flock of seagulls

I wish you would read the instructions first

so you don't jump in with both feet
thinking you can put things right
because life is not like that

there are parts you will always need to avoid

parts that are permanently broken
cannot be replaced
things that have been lost
some still pined over
things that do not work the way you
expect
some parts have a built in redundancy
a short shelf life

warning signs are placed
indications of what to avoid
diversions are in operation

so please note the signs
and do not trample on my grass

I'm fragile
breakable
and no amount of insurance
will cover me for
wear and tear

hospice

like Orwell's crumbs
the disturbed dust moves from
one surface to another
marking time in textured
layers

it covers all the people here as well

the room is cleaned,
the smells masked,
but the dirt is organic
it moves away from dusters
and vacuum heads
escaping to hang
in bars of light
and rest on people.

perhaps this is new dust
perhaps there is more dust here
because skin is dryer
hair looser more fragile
than outside where time still moves
in an understood way

I run my finger along
the dark oak mantelpiece
disturb a million lives
and learn to measure time
as the space between breaths

the stone

stones have slow thoughts
a static that can take an age
between each spark
as they
slowly wear to sand

a boy picks up
a white stone
that reflects the sun
he lets his finger follow
a dark line strata
inlaid a million years before
he takes it home
where it sits sixty years
as a memento
of a sunny day

the stone does not notice

beach

I count your ribs
finger walk
along the white boned way
follow with my tongue
the deltoid curve
of shoulder
to the sea salt of your ear
then trace the dunes of cartilage
along your spine
to a place we know,
and save for each other

my private beach
where every day is summer

Dockland

he was born in a dockland an age ago
he remembered the winters covered in snow
and the smell of the Boss White and verdigris
leaves breath like the wind through leafless trees
they're no more

he recalled the depression how he begged for his job
but the boss was a bastard and the foremen a sod
he had to join queues to get picked for a day
but often went home without any pay
they were treated like dogs

      he can still hear the sound of the one o clock gun
      that kept the ships true till their voyage was done
      now he sits at the Pier Head and gazes to sea
      and he remembers the stories and tells them to me
      tells them to me

he tells of the long walk to Birmingham
on the road that was trodden by many a man
and the promise of work that turned into dust
he worked where he could and did what he must
to survive

he remembers the ships that sailed from this port
and the ones he built and the ones that they fought
and the smell and the sounds of fire in the night
seeing his brothers going to fight
in a war

he can still hear the sound of the one o clock gun
that kept the ships true till their voyage was done
now he sits at the Pier Head and gazes to sea
remembers the stories and tells them to me
tells them to me

the salt in the water took skin from his neck
he was deafened by riveters up on the deck
and shouts could be heard from men down below
he hears them still and he's ready to go
they're calling to him

all the sounds and the smells of the Liverpool Docks
are still in his blood and hold him like stocks
he sits and remembers the things from his past
to him they're real but fading fast
they're fading fast

he can still hear the sound of the one o clock gun
that kept the ships true till their voyage was done
now he sits at the Pier Head and gazes to sea
remembers the stories and tells them to me
tells them to me

Dockland is a stage play with music which follows the lives of a family working in Liverpool Docks and ship building in the 20th Century. The play is loosely based on the life of Jim's father and this lyric is the opening song of the play and gives an overview of the story.

"What's your real job?"

"What's your real job?"
the little voice asked
from the second row
this is it I said
I get to come to schools
I write
"You in the library?"
someone shouted
some libraries
I said
"Crap ones."
someone suggested from the back
"And only when its raining."
another voice yelled

at this point
I was getting a bit defensive
I like my job
work hard at it
so I would never have to work
for a living
tried to explain
how writing and being a poet
is a job
it got a discussion going
so we talked about the jobs people do
and wrote a list

one girl said
"My dad used to work in the mines
but they stopped his job
so now he works in Asda."

Another kid told us
how his dad worked fixing cars
which impressed everyone
because they all got to shout out
the names of their favorite cars
"Has he ever drove a Lamborghini?"
"Bet he couldn't fix a Skoda

shell shocked at the end of the day
I left each of them
with a poem about their favorite thing
and a list of jobs that people do
it did not include "poet"

my critique of Rossetti

**Rossetti exhibition - Walker Art Gallery,
Liverpool – November 2003**

last week in Liverpool
I visited the Rossetti exhibition
at the Walker Art Gallery

someone had taken the trouble
to gather Dante Gabriele Rossetti's paintings
together and hang them on the walls

and there I was standing
watching waiting for the figures in them
to move or do something

but they don't they sit or stand
being beautiful and wearing masks
and they are not even who they say they are

these same women painted by him
captured a hundred times
in different clothes and paintings

twisting hands and hearts
the twisted genius tried to capture love
but instead left the dead mocking the living

in a mad moment
I took out my forbidden camera
stood casting a shadow

took a photo of my hand
fingers raised shadow cast
into his final work

a burning graffiti
that echoes in celluloid

visions

(1)
Archaeological Reminiscence of Millet's "Angelus".
by Dali 1935
(a poem for Hilary)

ripe from prayer two peasants
dance through a hundred reincarnations
in this one they are ruined architecture
bowed arched shapes

leaning on eternity

I am a figure in the foreground
holding or being held
unable to hear the noon bell
calling me to prayer

the bowed heads pray for us all

solid timeless figures
against our soft-time
sand-textured lives

(2)
Orwell in Wigan

time blown crumbs
move round the table
with the crockery

multiple covers layer the table
newspaper to protect the wood
old sheet to absorb the spills
cloth to hide the sins

and behind the waves of
couch bound adipose

a trapdoor to

darkness
beetle feet beat retreat
from mounds of flocculent tripe

brought out
laid out
spread out
coral on
the Welsh-slate slabs
a feast with peas

tell it like it was George,
if it ever was.

(3)
"Boulevard Monmatre, Spring 1897", by Pissaro

I could walk there
along
Boulevard Montatre
past the top-hated
men and long-dress and gowned ladies
accompanied by
the sound of horse hooves
beating on pressed earth

I could walk there
following the line of steady eye
and crafted paint
past spring tinted trees
shop fronts and houses on the hill
wander here and there
and sit and watch
as Pissaro must have done
and gaze at an horizon
curving to
the world beyond
that only he can see

(4)
Walk

I like to walk
along the ragged arse roads
between the tumble down walls
along the rubble rubbish strewn streets

walk, just that,
on dog splattered pavements
without a destination.

walk in an endless topography
on labyrinth paths
digging with my eyes
into shops and houses
other peoples lives
sucking in their life
like a baby on a teat.

bent-backed laboured lives
anonymous lives,
I stalk stories and poems
but always end up

writing about

myself.

pith

her nails dug through flesh and pith
released the scent of Californian groves
and made the orange smile

muse

3 a.m.
out of my
skull
I ripped my pants on a nail
in the alley behind the Irish Club

it happened
the rusty nail may still be there

rusting
till its all gone
drowning in a current
becoming a poem

the purpose of talking about poetry
is to talk about poetry
is to poetry and talk
and talk about talk
which is odd because what we don't do is talk
we make statements
electronic words sentences
sentencing us to wait for a reply.
I have no idea what it is about
or what it is about except poetry and talk
or talk and poetry.
I don't know
wish I did
there is an answer I am sure
I haven't found it yet
perhaps it lies
in defining the indefinable

understanding the unknowable
accepting that some things just are
or are not
or may be

rusting on the picket lines in Speke
speaking dead language poems
that inform on white boned miners
as black rock dust paints clouds over picket lines
or years later at Liverpool docks
waiting to be turned into myth
entropic rusting like a nail
poems speak to the contradictions

sell our newspaper in the street
take pennies from passing strangers
so children can eat
fade away the days
the docks
families at the docks
turning them to poems and myths
mythic poems
epics about myths
as if they never where

just words and poems
poems and words

poetry is structured talking or something
words stung together
hung together redefined in metaphor
strung up, hung up
strung up poems
written by strung up hung up poets
tyrants turning life into an art
so they can beat us with words

performance poets
performing
words and poetry
poetic words
bring a black art back into life.

but it's what it's about
it's steel and coal and lives
steel or rusty steel
it rips at you
and at 3am
in the alley
behind the Irish club
in Liverpool

poetry is a rusty nail

a poetry reading

I went to a poetry reading
a place where poets read their work
to other poets
waiting to read their work
heard a poet read a poem about a zoo
every animal was addicted to a drug
which was clever
because
some of the drugs
started with the same sound
as the name of the animal
like herons on heroin
anteaters on amphetamines
stuff like that
but the poem wasn't really about that

I find this with poems
they say they are about something
but afterward you realise
they are about something else.
the poem about the zoo
for example
was about a poet
being prepared to write anything for money
now that would be funny
except it was about something else
as well

I will probably read this poem
in a reading somewhere
people will wonder what it is about
only later will they realise
it was not about what they thought

the miracle

Simon takes the measured
polished wooden pieces
paints the joints with boiling wood-glue
from the workshop pot - it stinks of fish
places them on his bench
- blesses himself with the sign of the cross -
pushes them together and
wipes off the surface glue

later he holds it up admiring the shape
then returns it on his workbench
lips move to a silent prayer as
he takes a 30 centimetres cast
figure from a crate
blows off the polystyrene-ball packaging
and with care takes tacks and a small hammer
to nail Jesus to the wooden cross

on the last tap
the figures hand flies off
spins up
hits Simon in the face.
makes a small red mark

later people say
it was a miracle
he didn't loose an eye

poem?

they're supposed to be stories
I said
things I see
things that happen

yes he said
but they aren't poems
they don't rhyme or...

he couldn't find another thing
that made a poem a poem

they have short lines
I offered
they look neat sometimes

listen he said
this is a poem
(he quoted lines by
Blake)
yes
he said proudly
as he finished
this is a poem

yes it is
I replied
but so is this
I scribbled what he said
on a scrap of paper
he's watching now
as I write this
shaking his head
perhaps afraid to speak
in case he provides me
with an ending.

When Elvis came to Liverpool

in 1977 when he died
Elvis came to Liverpool
he was on his way to somewhere else
I don't know why but I know he came
perhaps it was just something he needed to do
I saw him walking along Church Street in the afternoon
turning up his high collar
against the Mersey breeze
later I caught sight of him in St Georges Hall
gazing at the mosaic floor
then I saw him at the Pier Head
heard him singing "Ferry Cross the Mersey"
to himself

a parade led by Elvis started late in the afternoon

it wound its way from the Pier Head
up past the Albert Dock
along Upper Parliament Street
past Gambia Terrace
and at a vantage point he stood for a while
looked down across the City rooftops
and listened to the bricks
that taught the 60's how to rock
then along Hope Street
past two cathedrals and back down into the town

more people joined the crowds that followed him

and all the while Elvis
sang quietly to himself
someone said later they heard him singing
"You'll never walk alone"
as he walked back down to the river
where he went out along the dockside
at the place the Isle of Man boat used to stop
climbed down a wooden ladder
then stepped out onto the water
he stood on the water for a little while
getting his balance
then he walked off across the River
towards the setting sun

the words of his last song
 "In my Liverpool Home"
drifting back on the wind

Allen Ginsberg's
Typewriter

Allen Ginsbergs Typewriter

Allen Ginsberg's typewriter

I bought
Allen Ginsberg's portable
Olivetti typewriter
from a pawnshop in Liverpool
where he had left it
on an Autumn day in 1965
(I had to pay a bit extra for it
because it had his initials,
along with others,
scraped into the paint on the base)

he had used it
to get a ticket to somewhere
where people wanted to listen
but never come back.

it's a funny thing
old fashioned and stiff keyed
needing Allan Ginsberg fingers to caress
the naked bone of the key top
and always typing in his voice

first I wrote a poem to my mom
but it turned in to a familiar poem
about someplace I had never been
then I tried again
it wrote a song to Father Death
and every time I tried to write
it wrote as he had done
until Howl was written

twenty times

I soon realised that it would only work for him
so I scraped my initials onto the base
and pawned it
I made sure I never went back
so unless anyone bought it
it is probably still there
looking out onto the world
through the pawnshop window
looking old now

with the money I paid the deposit
on a new typewriter
and a pair of scissors

gardeners

his fingers dig at the earth
lift up the sod
spade turns the soil
one blade at a time

bent backed
hunch shouldered
he who was my father
lives in this picture still

he writes pages in my book
and turns in memory
to smile and offer me
his soil stained hand

your father
I never knew
but I often gaze at his picture
on the sideboard in the hall

I can see them together
the two men
who labour in the garden
to clear a path for us.

poem for Woody

as you stand at night with your back to the wind
and hear the distant trains shunting
hear the heavy breath of labour
the cry of the new born and the gasp of the dying
in the harmony of life and death
it's there you'll find him
in chlorophyll stained dungarees
smelling of tobacco
riding the rails and singing
his words make you ache with longing
and his songs will make you cry
his voice is the voice of ages
and the voice is the voice of a lover
and the voice is the voice of an angel
that will lift you to the clouds and
he will show you how it all could be
and how it was
he will show you the injustice
he will make you feel ashamed
angry and indignant
he will point out a path towards justice and equality
but leave you to find your way alone
through public disaster and private grief
leave you standing with waves lapping at your feet
leave you lying watching unfamiliar ceilings
and unfamiliar faces making lakes and electricity
leave you to write the next verse and to carry on the song
that echoes with his name
and one day you will ask the questions he asked
and maybe you will get different answers
and maybe your answers won't be found in churches

or in a politicians rant
or in books or poems or vacant promises
maybe it is there just waiting to be heard
in the cry of a new born child
or the whine of a light plane
over Liverpool Bay
or at night when the wind blows

a poem for you

I want to write
a poem a milkman can whistle
on his round
I want to write
a poem to be printed on
a postage stamp
with one word missing
just to make each one valuable
I want to write
a humourous poem
one can sell on draft
in the pub
a barrel full of laughs
I want to write
a poem for you

at night when the world ends

there was a time when people believed
that at night the world ended
so many myths about it
the sun being eaten and born again
the day held by the powers of darkness
sacrifices and prayers
blood and effort
to birth the new day
make everything right

now in our cold bedroom
and my empty bed
I want to believe
that you will be there
when I wake
but there is no sacrifice
or effort I can make
no prayer that will work

and each morning
my heart is ripped out
held aloft
by your final words

camping on the mesa

it's night and I am standing alone now
the others long gone to their tents
the fires have died and I can feel the chill
but it is neither dark nor silent
there is an ambient light
and a shadow of an horizon
I imagine I hear nothing
but even in the silence there are sounds
the night breeze teasing grass
armoured insects, crashing, buzz and click
as they scuttle on the ground
and somewhere far beyond the Mesa
the plodding thump and squeal of a train

there are other sounds of course, human sounds
from the campsite, where tents stand, like spiders,
spread out across the boot churned field
snores, farts and the ripple of canvas
soaked and dripping from the evening rain
but they don't matter
they pass heard but unnoticed
in the deafening quiet.

here on the Mesa with senses night sharp
in this myth remembered dark and silent time
the world takes a breath.

monument

I can see a picture
wreckage of a building fascia
in a New York street
spread like angel wings
a monument
wrapped in a cloud
that shrouds the city
and hides
a wounded skyline

I hear the rhetoric
of sympathy and war
from faces lined with loss
as dust from New York
jet streams
across the world

you will find it everywhere
eventually
a dark cloud
on every horizon

writers group

I have my own
writers group
you would know the faces
of some who come
familiar from TV arts programs
you would recognize other names
from book covers

though some are dead
it does not prevent
their participation in this group
it is special
it is imaginary
and
it is mine

praise is forked
onto anticipated poems
waiting to be written
or the few lines of draft
in a notebook
but
the grandest words
are spent in praise
of the poem left on a bus
sometime in 1972
lost but always remarked upon
a remembrance
of a perfect piece
its loss the greatest tragedy
of literature

I used to belong
to someone else's writers group
I must have said too much
been too honest
because all those in the clique
began to criticise my poems
said how
odd they were becoming
how different
how peculiar

that was when I started my own group
invited only the best writers
Hemmingway, Bukowski and Dylan Thomas
raising a glass to my eloquence
Kerouac and Cassady
trying to get me to travel with them
Steinbeck crying over a line
John Fante, Updike and Braugtagan
a choir singing my praises
while Plath and Dickinson
argue over a word or two

but there are still problems
people snipe from outside
editors who go uninvited
reject my work
and at reading nights
people laugh at serious poems
like this

Wednesday

it must be Wednesday
the air is dry and smells of Wednesday dinner

from outside the slap of washing
like prayer flags twisting in the wind

from inside your distant song
accompanies your cleaning

I turn a page of my magazine
wondering about websites and making do

in the garden a bird sings
a Bob Dylan tune

the death of Pere Ubu

I dreamed of a poet who died today
his words strangled in my throat
left paper imitations
to tease us
like clouds on imaginary landscapes

I dreamed of an artist who died today
images in dust
hang on a plaster wall
pictures of a place
illuminated by his light

I dream of a man who died today
breathed his city one last time
and then is carried shoulder high
through crowds
who cry his name

I dreamed that Ubu died today

walking on the mesa

we walked out here
across the mesa
in the brilliance of night
and on the darkest of days
saw it crisp with frost
wet with dew
covered in cloud
and bright with summer
heard the birds
and the crickets
saw the flowers bloom
watched them
turn brown and die

now the first shoots
of the spring crocus's
are emerging in clumps
erupting
through the dark earth
the wintered trees
in-bud again
the cold air
once more
pregnant
with summer

the surprising thing
is that this
still happens
even though you
are no longer here
to see it

don't tell me

don't tell me
where you sleep
or who lies down
next to you

don't speak to me
about commitment
or time
or dead relationships
I don't want to hear
those stories
anymore

I don't want your dreams
or mine

all I want
is to have you beside me
in the morning
and to feel that you want me
here

satnd (stand next to me)

cmoe adn satnd hree nxte to me
yuo cna haer teh smuemr diyng
lesetn to teh tierd snouds of eevnig
as the cloo ari drifts through the gate

teh drkenass is aoslmt sliod
a wlal to kepe us in
or teh wolrd otu
I neevr culod fuirge otu wchih

bwron leeavs caerp asocrs teh pitao
warey ienstcs carek adn cclik
tiehr fainl wkees
adn I satnd hree wtaiing fro yuo
to be hree netx to me
as wrdos fial me

three parts of a hole

words are meaning - words are sight - part 1 of parts

a poem for Lawrence Upton

words are implied meaning
poets sort by enticing line from both
to which any is language
from ballads think with events
the road it comments on absorbed
which then perhaps dissolve
inanimate for themselves must pattern
words are sight
and those write words
give focus love comparisons
pace minute lyrical
that cut in from our edge

though the verse reflection
distinction narrative
close to a value what are about
the about a that doesn't form
and has the letter form
on and to the end extend poems
but was varying while characterising
my responses turns poet

form ends form
who poets with an effective tradition
emotional and potential concerns
to early over be significance
at poetic that fashions reading

is the is inverted create refined
posted heroic coherent straying
far from fluctuations
deliberate illumination
as they question being

Slow - part 2 of parts

sometimes he would try to die
cheat life of his spark
because he was a coward
he sat and willed his heart to stop
tried to dam the rivers pumping
in arteries and veins
he felt it
slow down
until
it
was
hard
ly
there

but it never quite stopped

he could probably be
encased in ice
for days then broken out
and be acclaimed
a guru
but that is not why he did it

his mental death was quick
but then his body just hung on

Collect - part 3 of parts

I collect words
and try keep them to myself
quietly going over them
in my head
some words scream at me
others whisper
and some times
they escape
grounded like lightening
through a pen

the cost of berries

August berries grow
on the hill overlooking the campsite
purple hand staining
juice mixes with the blood of the pickers
hands lashed
by the sharp bramble in the hedges

I am told
my mother cried that night called out my name
as tears ran through the sad crevices of her face

two hundred miles away
I sat under canvas
eating blood stained berries

Trevor's poem

Trevor stood
read his poem through
well grown beard

the union man
who had swum the English channel
butterfly
then wrung a poem
from the experience

spoke of the final mile
the longest one of all
and it became every challenge
of our lives

the final mile
the one we all face
on our own

mothers day

you are moving from the world
though some say you have already gone
I can see you lying in the box
with a false smile painted on your face
your blue lips red again

I know how much you hated
the small dark places
the thought of death
corruption and decay
so you will leave
in a flash of light
become a slick against the sky
and with the gentle touch of the breeze
moving in from the sea
drift like a cloud
towards the distant mountains

the dust of your passing
will lie forever
on the landscape of memory
a patina
that makes me what I am

remembering birthdays

I always remember your birthday
buy a card fill it out sign it
'with all my love, your son'
buy flowers
arrange them by the phone
thats about it really
flowers by the phone
for about a week
and for a week
when I come in
I am met by a floral scent
not unlike yours

on your birthday
I visit your grave
clean away the surface weeds
pull up the roots
dig out the tumours

I always remember
your birthday

I know things

I know how far away the sun is
how long it's light must travel
until it touches you
I know about clouds
and tides of air
when rain will come
to wash away your tears
I know about the turning Earth
and how time dissipates the grief

I know about death and finality
corruption and decay
pain and poverty
riches and plenty
and we've had them all

I know the turn of seasons
the unfolding of events
I know sometimes people
cannot see the lies
but that lies submerge you
in deceit

I know a lot
but I never know
what you are thinking

what is seen

```
     what     all you can write is what you see    what
     what is        you only write what you see       what is
   write what is        you only write what is        write what is
  you write what is        you write what is        you write what is
  you only write what is       write what is        you only write what is
  you only write what is seen       what is       you only write what is seen
 you can only write what is seen       what       you can only write what is seen
all you can write is what you see              all you can write is what you see
you can only write what is seen       what       you can only write what is seen
  you only write what is seen       what is        you only write what is seen
    you only write what is       write what is       you only write what is
     you write what is       you write what is       you write what is
      write what is       you only write what is       write what is
        what is       you only write what is seen       what is
        what     all you can write is what you see     what
```

A place I call England

A place I call England

A place I call England

there is a place in my head I call England
its green and rolling land fills up the spaces between grey hills
connected by lanes that wind between bramble hedges
tarmac coated lanes free to ride with only an occasional car
or tractor
lanes that drift into the past and disappear into the grass at
the roadside
lanes that meander through a countryside that smells of
scorching earth
and cow dung

in my England there are villages laid like Sunday tea
across manicured lawns
village greens with a pond where ducks and swans paddle
through the sunshine serenaded by church bells
I know it's like that
I saw it every Christmas on the box of chocolate biscuits
my mum bought home from the supermarket

although my view is of alleyway walls, towering brick,
and roads congested, stinking of cars, lorries and busses
and refuse which has been dumped on the playing field in the
night
as bins overflow and congeal
into a paper cardboard tin can mess in the entry
where houses lie empty and rotting for years
I know what England really looks like

(2)
my dad made a bit of England on an allotment
between the railway line and the factory
at weekends he would sit and plan his horticulture
cloche his beetroot tie up his runner beans
and with soil stained hands dig up potatoes
even though with every turn of soil he dug up bricks and tiles
it connected him to the land in a way he loved

(3)
There is a place in my head I call England
it has lived there all my life
and grows with every road I walk
every town I visit every city I come to know
It is populated with a thousand accents
a billion pictures of home full of life and colour
from snow topped hills rolling down its spine
to high-rise tower blocks street crime and grief
from slow time measured in seasons
to city time measured in seconds
I walk these roads and I call it home

Gatclif Road

I have forgotten the number
of the house
in Gatclif Road
but I remember the alcove
at the top of the stairs
in it were two doors
that were always in the dark
one opened into my bedroom
the other when nightmares
drenched the night
led to the comfort
of my parents room

across the landing
another bedroom door
which for years
was where my grandma slept
and then for years was empty
filled only with her smell
and a face that would visit me
in dreams

I remember waking
to a shaft of sunlight
as it cut through a curtain slit
getting up before anyone else
and in the living room
of the silent house
watch the fresh sunlight
of the early morning
sweep the dust
across the table top

each side of the window
built-in cupboards
always smelt of mustiness
made everything damp

I recall dry summer days
the garden smelling of mint
and the empty chicken run
which was my tardis
my place
where from behind the mesh
and in the cramped interior
I escaped to other worlds
and times
but always returned
to my own time machine
the one that moved me away from
each new memory
one day at a time

past-time

we drove along the lanes that Wordsworth walked
past lakes whipped into white tipped waves
past fields over which he strode for love
past gift shops flower shops tea shops
past bookshops selling the collected works
past his home his other home and hers

then to Dove Cottage and the obligatory tour
to see the things he lived with
to hear the sound of creaking beams he heard
to smell the plaster feel the wooden floor
to see a pen he wrote with
and a letter written at this desk

but in it all no sign of him
just spores left in his wake
he has gone heaved anchor
sailed off to find Arcadia

arrived home past nine
past time collating memories
then found him
lurking in a poem

celebrity death

stripping skin was the hardest thing
following the contours so it didn't rip
then scraping of the inner fatty tissue
stretching it to dry
carefully pinned out
to avoid shrinkage

smelling wistfully
it stood framed on its holding board
against the wall
attracting the glances of everyone
she would have loved the attention
the probing poking fingers
eyes that took in
the awed silence of her presence

later stuffed
and stood naked
in the celebrity area
hands touched her
as people passed
felt her hard cold breasts
caressed her groin
she kept smiling
they marvelled
this is the way to die they said
a sacrifice for your fans
true perfection
a real celebrity death

later people would hire her
to stand and greet guests
at their parties
and later still
when holes began to show
and thin skin exposed the stuffing
beyond repair
she was slipped away
into the basement
a quietly incinerated
her ash drifted out with the smoke
and left a trail across the sky

heroes

I saw a movie
the other night
a movie
about spacemen
who found an alien spaceship
they knew it was alien
because the spacemen
couldn't use the things
on the spaceship

seats wouldn't fit
doors the wrong shape
switches not made
to fit their hands
even toilets
that where impossible
to use
and everywhere
strange noises
and a gravity that made them
unsteady
and unable to walk

they felt out of place
looked out of place
as they fumbled round
in an heroically fumbley
out of place
sort of way
became the heroes
that everyone could cheer

brave men and women
learning to cope
with an alien environment

fantastic

of course in the real world
they would have given them
a blue badge
a patronising smile.

concrete

I hear words
broken words
detached from their meaning
haphazard phrases
used without thought
casually
as if meaning has no meaning

put the kettle on
I can't it doesn't fit
run the bath
it never moves

it makes no sense to me
I was born with concrete
in my head
as rational and solid
as a brick

I spent hours
trying to figure out the world
waiting for trees to bark
and for the cow
that lived next door
to come out

put the telly on
turn the telly over
Nothing makes any sense

after a visit to London when all had gone well

black beetle taxies crawl curbs
while crushed glass voices
shriek for attention
an underpass opens legs wide
sucks in the worms
excretes congestion
onto constipated streets
that stink of death

outside, the river
wind churned turns
grey
bridges lines against
the blue black sky
birds on bankside
peck for crumbs
suspend on wind currents
then drop swallowed
by the river
erupt
waterspray and blood
back into the air

spit stained pavements
drip into gutters
umbrellas joust
people mouths moving
speak
or want or wait to speak
or dribble
beg unnoticed
for attention
poster colours run down walls
eye suck advertising
screams about an exhibition
of surreal art at the Tate Modern

razor blades at eyes
sharp enough to cut you
I don't think I'll go

landscape

after shopping at Tesco's
built between
landscaped landfill hills
we struggle to get all our
plastic shopping bags
card crates of cans
and bottled water
in the car boot space

our shopping spills over
onto vacant seats
into footwells
we manuvour
soft fruit, eggs,
cracker packs
to the top

all the time we
talk about poetry
and what we
leave
for prosterity

bones

lay my back bone
bleached white
beneath a waterfall
to be rubbed scrubbed
by endless
weight of water
into tiny
marble-stones

set my feet upon the road
and let them wander

wash out the jelly
memories
from my head
and place my skull
in tree roots
to become a home
for little thoughts

then set my feet upon the road
and let them go

place an arm and hand
protruding from the earth
point it homeward
when the wind blows
from a distance it will seem
I wave goodbye

now set my feet upon the road
it's time to let me go

sunsets

in photographs
all sunsets look the same
red sun sinking into night
but I have seen so many
and all of them are different
you cannot photograph
the way it makes you feel
but you can feel that way
when you look at the photograph
even if it looks
like a thousand other sunsets
but if you put that sunset
on a billboard
it is just another sunset
to everyone
apart from you

you cannot photograph
death
smells
anger
pain
or starvation
you can photograph the effect
you can show stick figures
frozen as they walk aimlessly
towards their death
put that on a poster
post for everyone to see
till it becomes
just another figure
walking to their death
and it's just like another sunset
to everyone

but it isn't is it?

dawn

I don't wake now;
I lie and listen to the silence.

ten years ago
at dawn
I would wake
as birds began
a hundred songs
mixed to a choir

and I would lie half wakeful
for a while
pick out the individuals
then doze
as a sun drenched sky
stirs up the day sounds
and mixes them in

now I wake at dawn
without a sound
and lie awake
listening to the silence
and wonder
 what it means

holiday postcards

we are writing postcards
at a café table
overlooking
Lake Windimere
I write this one to you
and I know
you will just laugh
when you find it
waiting on the mat
at home
because
I can see you
writing your postcard to me
later we will post them
hidden in the pile to our friends

a holiday is like that

some people
bring home with them
others do their best
to leave it behind
me I write postcards
to remind myself
of the moment
when you smile at me

See

I see he said
as he stares through screwed up eyes
and plays two handed with his glasses
(lenses thick as tiles)
I think he meant the other sort of see
the sort that doesn't see or rather
sees only what it wants to see
the sort that tries to twist and make
something else of what is said
so that it fits his view
of how things are
or should be
the unfocussed stare attempts to fix
the image he imagines;
the poor sad soul
who lost his mother so many times
and loses her again each night
and all that that brings with it.
pointless trying to tell him that I didn't care
pointless because he believes I must
pointless because
he wants to make me care
to reach inside my head
and rearrange the things in there
but I can only feel his blindness
as he gropes in the dark

steps

the stone steps worn away
sway in the centre
through years of feet
tearing at them
and in the cracks
weeds and grass
try to gain a hold

then this guy
uninvited tolls me about
his mothers death
how he said
her lungs burst
because she smoked too long

I throw my ciggie
onto the steps
turn my foot on it
see a black streak
left behind
wonder how long
that will be there

then the guy tolls me
about his brother
who blew out his brains
no none knew why

I take out a ciggie and light up

snapshot 2

tiny ice crystals
fill the mackerel sky
with cirrocumulus
build toward a storm later

on the river
ships pipe 1 pm.
as brief rays of sunlight
spotlight the rooftops

I listen watch feel
for the first drops of rain
as the clothes on the washing line
billow in the freshening breeze

the dogs can sense the storm
hide somewhere indoors
while the garden mower
stands unmoving

I watch from the patio doors
cup of tea in one hand
microphone in the other
it is 1.05
and I can feel the first
drops of rain

snapshot 3

someone is cooking fish
I hate the smell
it must be a barbecue
I can hear them
shouting in whispers
as the dog stained grass
struggles to recover
I don't think I can stay here
the smell will ruin my lunch
"here" is the patio
"here" is my back-garden
here trees block neighbours views
mitigate the sunlight
turn the suntrap of the brochure
to a dappled inconsistency

a bird eats
from the feeder
hanging from the shed gutter

in the next garden
the fish burns

snapshot 4

the blue glass bowl
turns light into cloud pictures
on the kitchen table
waiting for the kettle to boil
watch the steam turn
against the ceiling
tap drips

as kitchen boiler
bubbles into life
Monty sits up
waiting for my hand
to reach for his lead

flowers blooming in the rain
as bags of pebbles
wait to look like
something Japanese

Eureka Cafe (1970)

pushing weight against gravity
over Llandegla moors
then descend pedal free
down Horseshoe Pass
past open mines
and shingle reefs
past huts and houses made from slate
past railway and Iestedford site
to stop for lunch
on rocks at white flowing rivers side

later turning peddles
back through Worlds End
light drizzle on the air damp
soaks through
cycling kit to skin.
gripping tight to bars
on the clenched teeth climb.
through forest on to open moor
then plunging down again
to Wrexham and the main road home.

a final stop at Two Mills,
Eureka Cafe beans
draped over toast
while cyclists exchange stories
of summer tours
 races won or lost

as they steam
contentedly in the warmth.

the living room

in the living-room
of my old family home
the light purple paper
with the blocks of abstract flowers
clings on with the tenacious paste of years
finally succumbs
to water and my scraper
when the steamer arrives

underneath
onion layers
reveal the yellow flowers
of my teenage years
fresh again
flowers that looked down
as I deflowered Emily
on the couch
peal back
to the thin blue stripes
of childhood
and on down to others
I have never seen

a yellow green
with the trellis lines
and climbing
vines of mum's early
married years
then brown with age
the final layer
the last sight of home
my granddad had
before he went
to war and death

too many layers
soaked and stripped
fall round my feet
as walls
stripped of their history

wait to start again

trouble at Tesco's

I didn't realise anything was wrong
until I saw the tin of beans.
it was a large tin of Heinz baked beans
not the Tesco own brand type
that I prefer most
on a single round of toast
these beans
where the wrong beans
they may be right for other people
but not me and no one comes to share
a large tin anyway
so it would go to waste

so when I realised I had the wrong beans
I started to check all the items in the trolley
there was some pasta
but it was the thin quill shaped tube
I would never use
it would take too long to look inside each one
I only use the sort that look like seashells
and give no hiding place
and there were sausages as well
and other things that I would never eat
Cornflakes
and a pack that makes crème caramel
creamy Channel Island milk
spaghetti hoops
dried noodles tied in loops
and tins and packets of
unpronounceable foreign-sounding soups

it was clear then
someone had stolen my trolley
and left this impostor in it's place
filled with counterfeit food
the stuff I do not like
and which would probably make me ill
it might even be designed to kill

I knew what I had to do

someone had taken my trolley
highjacked my food
someone had it.
so I set out to find it
stalking through the isles and checkouts
looking through peoples trolleys
for my kidnapped food
people looked worried
when I told them
"watch out" I said "look after your trolley
someone's stolen mine."
They looked alarmed
when I told them
some even ran off
guarding their trolleys to the checkout

at last a helpful policeman came to help
I told him what had happened
He nodded sagely
took a look in the trolley
noted the details in his book
but before he could arrest anyone
a manager brought my trolley back
said he'd found it by the photo booth

where I go and sit sometimes
when people start to look at me
but I knew it was a lie
he must have had it all along
I looked at him
memorised his thin smiling face
and twitching eye
for future reference

then the policeman pushed my trolley
as we took it through the checkout
and waited outside for the bus
to take me home

it's a good thing, living in the community
but not when people steal your trolley

Down in Liverpool

Down in Liverpool

down in Liverpool

(1)
Last night I managed to get rid of a lot of my problems,
Quite easy really, I got so drunk I couldn't remember
What the problems were or even if I had one in the first
place.
This morning I clawed my way out of bed,
And stuck a bare foot down on a moist and chunky mat.

Then I smelt the smell of last nights vomit
Puked some more and felt better for it.
Fresh is always easier to clean.
I could hear Jane, "You'll die you arsehole."
That's what she always said.
She was right of course, but not today,
That will be some other day.

I can't face the cleaning, it is a waste of time anyway.
The carpet by the bed has begun to go into a hole,
Either through stomach acid in the sick that hit the same
spot,
Or through Jane's and my attempts to clean it up.
Or maybe something else wore the holes there.

When Jane had first been here, we had often made love in
the day
On the mat in front of the window.
Her on hands and knees her dress lifted at the back
Me erect behind her
My head and upper torso above the level of the window sill,
Grinning like a lunatic at people walking by.

She said I would loose all my teeth
Perhaps like Mrs Pickup from downstairs
I found Mrs Pickup one morning lying outside
Her face glaring at the sky, the first dead body I had seen.
At first I had not realised that it was Mrs Pickup from
downstairs
Then I did and I was shocked by the absence of teeth
I mean I knew she was dead,
But her face was all sucked in like a sex doll
And there was no life
What was left was just vacant space
Filled with a body that looked a bit like she used to.
But without teeth.
She had this funny look on her face like surprise.
Not shock or pain just surprise.
So if her life was not quite fixed,
At least it was less broken than it used to be
And it couldn't get any worse.

So Jane had said I would loose all my teeth and that scared
me
Because the acid would eat my teeth away
Eat my
teeth
away
like
the
Carpet.
I don't brush my teeth if I do I bleed for ages, if I brushed,
So I swill out with salt water, polish, swill clean what I can
Polish with the end of a sheet which
Somehow had started getting used as a towel. A bed sheet
towel.

So I start another day.
Climb into some clothes which are just wearable

Open the window, Leave it open to clear the stink
And wade out into the world to get some breakfast.
And some more booze before I begin to forget to forget
Whatever the problem was.

If there was one.

(2)

I walked down the street towards town
Past the student housing, with its windows wide
And blaring mix of radio and CD players
And scream-singing-talking students hanging out of windows
And a three chord guitar player singing about some place
He'd heard about in other peoples songs but never seen
All above the row of shops
All mixing into a frantic dub-reggae-jazz, pop-folk-rock song
Past the chippy with its polystyrene tray and chip paper
garbage
Blowing in the doorways
And its yellow stained curried pavement
Curried ground chipped
        pavement
Past the newsagent with its boarded windows and piles of
milk crates
Past the Philharmonic Hall with flapping flags
Beating against paint pealing posts
Down and down and down to Liverpool

(3)
My geography of Liverpool is marked out by bookshops
Second hand shops, cheap breakfasts,
And places where things happened

Ye Crack where Jane and I drank on Sunday's
The Odd Spot, the Legs of Man
The steps at St George's Hall where I cried for John
And sang a pop song that became a secular hymn
And where I sang it for Jane before the police told me
I was drunk and had to be quiet and move on
And Lewis', the phallic symbol of Liverpool
Now looking limp and dangling like a dead fish

There is so much of us in this place

(4)
The stupid brown tray started to shake as soon as I picked it
up
And as I tried to walk to a table it got worse
everyone was looking at me
It got worse and the floor was sticky so I couldn't walk
I walked like a joke drunk
Someone took the tray, put it on a table in the corner
Said something, left me
The tray sat still on the table so I tried to eat
But ever time I picked up my food it started to shake
So I had to put it down

It must be nearly drinking time

That's what happens when its nearly drinking time
Everything starts to shake till drink makes the world stand
still again
After I eat some I stood up and walked out
Managed to keep it down until I got out
Then threw up in a waste bin in Church Street
I could hear Jane, "You'll die you arsehole."
Maybe she was right
But not today.

(5)
The night before she left
She stood up and fumbled with the fastener on her jeans
Pulled them down to her knees underwear as well
Stood in front of me,
For the first time I noticed her pubic hair had turned grey
She rubbed her hand across it making sex noises
I thought that was funny I laughed and she laughed
Then arranged herself on the mat bottom waving in the air
She made more encouraging noises, tried to sex herself
Then I started laughing again
She gave up
We tried later but it was no good
I just dangled like a dead Liverpool fish.

Sometimes when I think about it
I think that was our last supper
a failed attempt at communication
But I could never understand why she wanted sex
The night before she killed herself.

I could hear her, "You'll die you arsehole."
Maybe she was right
But not today.
Today I will get drunk before I start to remember
Whatever it is I'm trying to forget.

war is

war as Mr Johnson said
is a bastard -
I supposed he must know
he had left his arm
on a battlefield
and thought he was lucky -
perhaps he was -
he used to tell stories
to anyone who'd listen
how he'd volunteered
and lay sinking in mud
alongside the distorted faces
of the soon to be dead
and the corpses
that were left to rot
into the ground

I remember how
on special days
he wore bits of faded
shrinking uniform
and pinned his empty sleeve
like a medal
to his shoulder

twenty years later
I was amazed
when the man on one side of me
had his arm torn off
by an IRA bomb
leaving a look of disbelief
while on the other side of me
a bolt tore through
another mans face
and his head opened like
over ripe fruit
between them I stood untouched
except for the blood and brain
which ruined my jacket

but then as Mr Johnson said
war is a bastard

stumble

I walk round you
even though
you're no longer there
I thought
I knew where
you would always be
but only found you gone
when I stumbled
put my hand out
and no one took it

picking up the pieces

"Don't waste my life." she screamed
I spat in her face to make her wild
"Too fucking late." I yelled

That's how it was
anything could be disputed
anything

And always afterwards
victims
lay about the room

Today it was
the blue and white
roasting dish
smashed by a badly aimed
or just avoided
beer bottle

She looked in horror
at the thousand pieces
spread across the room
the last remaining
wedding present

broken

"I'm going out." I said
"I can't stand crying women."
I slammed the door behind me

left her sitting
crying trying
to pick up the pieces.

skin deep

as we make love
he loiters in those corners
which will never be mine
dawdles on the skirting edge
lingers on the top of a wardrobe
while my cloths dangle
across a chair back

a discarded bus ticket
from a journey he once took
found between the pages of a book
the special pan he cooked noodles in
and a luminous kipper tie
forgotten in the bottom
of your washing basket

and always he lies down with us
alive
inside your closed eyes
as he screws you again

dream

I once dreamt a girl
who stayed with me through
nights and days of sleep
cat naps and forty winks
she was always waiting
arms ready to
embrace me
mouth eager
to be kissed
I was the real-world fantasy
that fulfilled her ambition
to be more than
a dream.
while
she was my
dream wife succubus

one day I woke
and found her lying next to me
mouth ready
to complain
and once she began
she never stopped

now sleep is where I go
to escape from her

regret

she said it was time to go
before the drink had more effect
and before she would regret
whatever it was she might regret
if she didn't go
or if she waited till morning
and only left when
rattled milk bottles woke her.

she said it was time to go
and thanks for the booze
but it didn't buy her body
she was, she said, a free spirit
waiting to see the dawn rise
rooftop high
and hear birds singing
she would walk she said
along the empty streets till light

she left twenty years ago
and as she left a riot started
along the road
that night I watched as fires
lit up the sky like war
reflecting on the dark slate roofs
now there are no milkmen
and the birds don't sing
but I regret that I will never know
if she had lived to regret it.

the last groove

the plates drip dry
cups up-turned drain
as water runs in rivulets
into the sink
smoke escapes
from the chimney
of the house
across the garden
while black birds forage
pull up worms
from moist
new turned soil
music is playing somewhere
but for now
my revolution is over
the sterile CD unscratched
version of the Pistols
has come to an end
but I miss the sound
of a stylus
playing the last groove
forever

Church Street

on Sunday we went to Church Street
window shopping nursed hangovers
looking in at windows
that pretended to be rooms
in Lees, rooms
filled with furniture and pictures
vases and cardboard books
clean window rooms arranged to live in
but without people

Jane wondered who could live in little rooms
filled with furniture and pictures,
vases and cardboard books and all of them
with labels and printed signs
that would get in the way or stick in you
if you wanted to stretch out with a can of beer
or something
and I could see what she meant

I liked the colours there is an excitement
in new furniture and a smell a new smell
like carpets or cars or babies a unique new smell
that is forever-after *that* place
even when the smell has gone
even if you smell the smell someplace else
it reminds you of that other place,
that place that smelt new
when it was new
before the smell disappeared
or we stop noticing it
and before the room began to smell of us

unseen

the unseen wreckers
got there before me
turning out drawers and cupboards
breaking crockery
pursuing treasure
and shitting on the carpets

for the first time
I was glad you were dead

but they only took things
which didn't matter;
a little money left in your purse,
chequebooks to closed accounts,
a tv and video,
things you never cared for

and strewn across the floor
they left behind
the things you loved:;
the pictures from your wedding day
of you and dad
at the start of life
your cup, chipped but still intact
the pictures of a baby that was me
and all the worthless
treasure of a lifetime

left strewn across the floor
like leaves in the autumn
a patchwork counterpane
collage of life

the car parked in your drive

I saw the car
parked in your drive
a green one
with the broken lights
and smashed windows
some things you can't keep bottled up
some things
you have to write about
so I wrote this poem
about the car in your drive
but the driver was not in the car
it was not being driven
and with broken lights
and windows
it would have let the rain in
and the driver would not have been able
to drive it very well
but the driver was elsewhere
and so where you
but the green car was in your driveway
and I was outside
watching the shadows
play like puppets on the bedroom blind
and his car in your driveway
with broken lights and windows

they weren't always
broken of course
but my solicitor has advised me
not to talk about that

pronouns and tenses

I who was we
am converted into pronouns
property lists
agreements
minutes and memos
and all the other legal
paraphernalia of the living
and in every one
I am
written about typed and
spoken of
in the past tense

she
the wife
of the first part
is wrapped in argument
comforted by condemnation
and generally
makes demands
that she knows
can not be met

but then I
the husband of the second part
just want to be free
to get on
be myself again

for a silly moment I thought
that was what she wanted too

the worm world

on the surface the soil is warm
sun dried and dusty
coats my hands grey
but when I dig down
turn a spade full
expose the dark cold
worm world
it frightens me

bushes and trees
dig down deeper than me
churn up the soil
push it aside
pump up the moisture
somehow
they find comfort in it
perhaps they cannot think about
or see the decay
in which they grow

the hole we dig grows deeper
longer than its width
down into the darkness
down into the bone chill earth
down into the worm world
where everyone sleeps at last

PC

it has been a while since I wrote anything
the moods been wrong
the place
the familiar bits of life are missing
it's always like this
when I move on
but this isn't what I planned
and if I got everything from her house
I wouldn't have anywhere to put it

I couldn't put the PC in here;
if the roaches didn't eat it
then kids would have it for their next fix

I tried to make it feel like home
bought some books
propped them up against the wall
but threw them out
when little things
began to eat the pages

I let the empty beer cans
stand idle untouched on
shelves and table
it gives the place a scent
that hides the smell of puke

I can imagine my empty den
waiting for me to fill it
and start writing
words coming from
fingers pounding on the keyboard
while here all I have
is a pencil
to point out the inconsistency
of being a writer who cannot write

the man who hugged clouds

The man who hugged clouds

where poetry is

you want me to tell you where poetry is?
ok it's in the inconsistencies
that hide between lines
like the incoherent mumbles of the drunk
or the rambling of the sick and dying
it's in the last moments of the sunset
and the first light of dawn
it's noon and midnight
the echo of a train
the sound of children playing
it's in the cry of despair at loss
and in the sky punch exaltation of success
it flies with the birds
pinned against the sky
swims with fish
floating on endless currents

it's in shops
on posters and handbills
tins and packages
signs and billboards
you will hear it in a theatre in Crosby
in a cinema in Birkenhead
or in the third room at the Everyman Bistro
it's in the ripples of the dessert
and on the mountainside
it's in the song of a busker
in a pedestrian underpass
by St johns market
and the breeze that moves the grass
like an endless ocean

it's in the temptation of a warm still night
the linking touch of two bodies
the smells of toilets
the stench of vomit
and the flow of blood after an accident
and its in words
single simple words that stand for themselves
and spatial words
that take us someplace else

it's in the black endless
colour of night
in the silver of the moon
as it sparkles
on wet leaves
the swish of tyres on wet tarmac
on a motorway going
somewhere
and on a road going
nowhere
that cuts through the night
with arc light brilliance
it's in the opening of a flower
the closing of a door

and in your eyes

and really it's everywhere if you look for it
and nowhere if you don't

being Bukowski

my friend recently said
that he was going to become
Bukowski

so I bought him a bottle of whisky
to get him started

a month later
he was still living
in his bought-and-paid-for house
going out for Sunday pub lunch
shopping at Asda

I asked about his father
he told me that he still missed
the lovable old goat
wasn't he a Nazi I asked
oh no he said he was a Tory
lovely guy
left happy memories
of a happy childhood

oh well I said at least
you will have had crap jobs
you could write about those
when you descend
into drunken oblivion
and the gutter
but no he'd been in a job he loved
all his life

so how is the
becoming Bukowski going
I asked
great he said and produced
pages of scribbled poems
from his attaché case

they weren't Bukowski
they were just my friend
trying to become
Bukowski

two short poems....

clouds

if clouds were made of candy floss
I would be at a total loss
to explain
rain

counting

I used to have trouble counting
I used my fingers and toes
but then I discovered binary
so now I only use my nose

the book

I was too tired to read
the book lay broken-backed and flaccid
on the hotel bedside table

sometime in the night
a stray leg must have kicked it to the floor
maybe it slid and hid under a corner unit

when we packed it lay undisturbed
and then went unnoticed on the final check
we left without it

now although I'll never know what happens
the ghost of the book still marks its place
on the library shelf

gazing

I saw a naked man
looking at me
from a bedroom window
I think he was naked
but he may
have been wearing
pajama bottoms
or shorts
or trousers or something
I couldn't tell
I could only see
the bit that was in the window
and that was naked
then a lady came
and stood beside him
and she was naked too
so then they where both
gazing down at me
as I lay in the gutter
gazing back
at her round firm breasts
that were also gazing down
at me
with nipples
sticking out like thumbs
then she leaned forward
and her breasts
squashed against the glass
like two cartoon eyes
with tiny pupils

I know I should
have tried to get
the number of the car
that knocked me off my bike
but at the time
it didn't seem
important

fridge poem

I try to write poems
wherever I am
out walking or jogging
or in a traffic jam
and now I have letters
stuck to the freezer door
and i write poems until
i don't want to write anymore
but i have twO problems
wrtng ths way
the frst s that new pOems
wpe Old Ons away
and th 2cond
tht Befr vry lng
1 run ut f Lttrs
a cn fn N g

the eponymous hero of my life

the eponymous hero of my life
is tall slim with black flowing hair
sometimes long
sometimes tight cropped
always heroic

always saying the right thing
at the right time
always admired
always right

he stands up for political
legal and social justice
as he fights for the rights of individuals
against the grinding machine of state

he is a role model
to all around him
a magnificent sportsman
who won the football world cup
in black and white
the rugby world cup
with the final kick
in full living colour
several test matches against Australia
bore the Ashes home in triumph
won the Tour de France
after 21 grueling stages
that brought him to the brink of defeat
saw him struggle on mountain passes
almost crash out

then rise again
in a fearsome attack
that won the day

the eponymous hero of my life
watches a lot of TV

fluttering

I saw a wing fluttering
in the road
thought I could help
but it was just a wing
glued to the ground
by guts and blood
feathers
moving in the breeze

I had to move to the pavement
as other cars came
wheels drove over it
squashed it
flat to the ground
but after they had passed
the wing rose again
and started fluttering

in imitation of life.

this afternoon

This afternoon
        passed quickly
        I took out subscriptions to three poetry magazines
        then cancelled them
        read a Basil Bunting poem and finally understood it
        then read it again and realised I didn't
        I started reading War and Peace
        but then decided I should start a note book and
        collect ambiguous statements
        like -   "laced up stout boots to walk the dogs then
        remembered I didn't have any"
        and your absolute classic - "I really do love you"
This afternoon
        I sorted out two jigsaws, separated straight edges
        from the rest
        then hid the corner pieces down the chair to save
        time
        I wrote an essay entitled a hundred ways to pass an
        afternoon but gave up after
        Number 1 Write an essay
        wrote three improvisational plays with the same
        instruction "be yourself"
        and discovered a cure for people who think they
        know it all
        but I forget what it is

This afternoon

    I sat at the end of the road and wrote down the
registration numbers of passing cars
counted the birds who balanced with eaves-dropping
feet on the telephone wires
launched myself three feet into space from the
garden wall
listened to all the CD's you left on that strange mode
that changes tracks after 10   seconds
then heard Lady in Red and knew why that mode
exists

This afternoon

    I worked out that I could change the channel on my
TV quickly enough to see   three chat shows at
the same time.
heard about two cases of people who had
relationships with people it turned out they didn't
know -
and three cases of people who had relationships with
people they did know but who didn't know them
very well

This afternoon

    kicked a plastic bowl round the kitchen, won the
footbowl world cup
got the mower out to cut the grass smoked it instead
        (another one for my ambiguous notebook -
and another)
I started making dinner for one then decided to get a
sandwich from the shop
sometime

This afternoon

    passed quickly
now I sit and wonder why I didn't have this much
fun when you where here.

the rock

sand compacted into stone made this rock
and somewhere in the centre of the rock
history is trapped
locked in a universe where
only it can tell itself

between grinding fingers
65 million years of effort is turned to
d

u

s

t

poem – this is not a poem

you may think this is a poem
but it isn't
I don't write poetry anymore
I prefer to spend time
it is a currency
which is finite
more suited to my existence
than
the infinite possibilities of words

keeping count

death met them as they left the train
kept the count
as it strode along the platform
in its sharp creased uniform

it sat at tables making a selection
it gathered in the clothes
it mounded up the glasses
extracted teeth
poured in the gas
pulled out the dead
burned up the corpses

death kept count
of the soon to be dead
till they became
more marks on a sheet

it filled up graves
with them
and with the dust of millions
as it tried to keep the count

afterwards death said
it had just been
obeying orders

imaginary words

in maths I can imagine numbers
imaginary numbers, a little i
designed to resolve a conflict
in the square root of 1

my square root is
round the houses
without words to share with you
i make imaginary words
and paste them in my eyes.

i hope that they resolve
the conflict.

banshee

she's in the corner now
pursuing darker thoughts
straining to see the crack of light
between the bricks
it will open into the other place
she says a safe place

I know it doesn't exist
but she is convinced
and pursues her witchcraft
through the night
to combat that
which only she can see

sometimes she stands
on the dark landing
steering into the cracked mirror
she swears she sees
the souls of the dead
their faces painted on her own
and she says she hears
the screams of the banshee
calling my name
but I hear nothing
and see only her reflection
and mine

gaze
a poem for Roger Cliffe-Thompson

he has been into the grey distance
where mountains partition Earth and sky
climbed the muscle-aching slopes
into the clouds
and gazed back to this place
and wondered what it was like

he has been into the hidden places of the Earth
burrowed deep into its skin
through caves and tunnels
down precipitous falls
and up escarpments few have seen
to claw his way back into life

no one knew
he kept his history tight
but I could see it
written in his eyes

shooting pigeons with your fingers

in 1964 Billy Blackstock
fingers held like a gun
was playing at shooting pigeons
as he shouted "BANG"
a pigeon fell down dead

I saw Billy last week
and like every other time since then
he points his finger
like a gun and shouts "Bang"
and just like every other time
I say "Glad your aim's no better"
and somewhere in the chat
we talked about that bloody bird
again

I realized then that he has been
trying to fire his finger now
for over forty years

another guy I know
once found three half crowns
wrapped up in a five pound note
spoke about his good fortune
long after the money was spent
and ever since kicks at
paper and moves pavement rubbish
with his toe.
worse perhaps

he walks head down
scowering pavements
just ahead
for the tell tale signs
of treasure
he thinks he is the luckiest guy on earth
finding pennies most days
and always telling people
how lucky he is

I'm glad I never shot a pigeon
with my finger
or found a treasure trove
on a pavement
I don't think I could stand
 the pressure

me I wrote a poem for my mum
she loved it
showed it to all her friends
for all the years before her death
would tell of how
I once wrote a poem for her

that was years ago
and I often think how odd it is
that a moment
years before can echo through a life

History

usually history detaches itself from me
creates its own time
punctuated by significant events
it becomes part of an ageless memory
things read, heard about or observed
when I try to name historical events
I recall things like Kennedy's assassination,
Lennon's murder and the shuttle explosion

I never think of the fall of the wall
the end of oppression
or the other good things that happen
for me it's death
that marks time

but I use private events
to measure my life;
seeing you for the first time,
holding our children
as they were born,
sharing their lives
remembering the things
they will forget
these are never linked to history
they are just our story

but occasionally history intrudes,
involves me as an observer
draws me in and makes me part of it
now in slow motion
I dream of two towers burning
watch it play out again
and again and again
unable to forget
it is lodged
between taking the children to school
and you coming home
it sticks, timeless,
held in my life
a fixed point
like a bullet in the head

Walking on the Beach with Charlie

Charlie my poodle
is walking beside me
trotting over the dunes
filling his hair with wind
as my shoes fill with sand
and we screw eyes
against the gusting grit

children descend
on flattened cardboard boxes
sliding over tufts of grass
and on and down
propelled by shrieks
onto the beach below
I can see Charlie looking
wondering if he could have a go
deciding against it
with a sniff

now we sit
Charlie comfortable
head on my knee
locks eyes with me
and I tell him of the journey
we will take together
of Steinbeck
and another Charlie
years ago
and with unspoken wisdom
he tells me about love
with a glance

Rumours

as I stopped at the park gates
Buckowski's book fell open
on a crack backed page
a page that held a poem
about a soldier, his wife
and a bum
I read the poem
as Charlie waited patiently

it makes me think about war
they way Buckowski must have
when he wrote it

we are on the verge of war again
everyone is thinking about war
wondering where it will lead
most people don't want it
but we will do it anyway

like we know smoking gives you cancer
but we still smoke

from up on the hill
I watch Charlie running round
digging in the sand dune roots
and biting at the wind

before we came out
someone said there was war in the air
but here without the commentary
I can only taste the salt

flocculent

you gave me a fleece coat
a present at Christmas
I didn't realise how cold I was
until it made me warm

the great adventure

there is a road that leads from there to here
some of it rocky some smooth
with hidden twists and turns
diversions and dead ends

it leads over hills
and almost impassible mountains
descends rushing like a crystal stream
through sweet vallies
and carries on, sweat stained,
into filthy gutters

eventually it brought me here to you
where our two roads crossed
and now it tugs us on
towards the great adventure
that lies ahead

The Man who Hugged Clouds

the man who tried to hug clouds
succeeded one day
he said he was no longer
the man who tried to hug clouds
from that moment
he was the man who hugged them
and he loved it
rolled in the sublime wetness
of the hug
took clouds into himself
became closer than
he had ever thought possible

he would never say how he did it
but would smile when asked

one day after a thunderstorm
he could not be found
and although everyone searched

he was never seen again

About The Author

Jim was born and still lives near Liverpool in England. He grew up in Liverpool during the years of the Mersey Sound and the Liverpool Poets and it is from this tradition that he developed his own unique style and voice.

He is the author of 53 books including books of poetry, books for children, and technical training manuals. In addition his CD "Down in Liverpool" a selection of poetry and music has brought Jim to the notice of a much wider audience. In a career spanning 35 years Jim has won many accolades for his performances and writing. Recent awards include;

Silver Stake for Performance Poetry (2001)
Fante Prize for Literature (New Mexico 2000)
Poetry Super Highway Poet of the Year 2000.
Sefton Literary Competition prize winner.
San Francisco Beat Poetry Festival Competition, 1st prize and Judges Choice - October 2002

His poetry has been widely published in magazines and anthologies and he regularly performs at poetry events and festivals in the UK and USA. Jim runs courses in Creative Writing for the University of Liverpool, Edge Hill University College and for the Workers Education Association. In September 2002 Jim was selected to represent Liverpool as part of the successful bid to become European Capital of Culture 2008.

At the first DaDaFest Awards Ceremony in December 2003 Jim won two prestigious awards the first as Best Established Artist and the second as Best Individual Performer.

In February 2004 he was appointed managing editor of the poetry information site poetrykit.org.

He is available for readings and workshops in Schools, events and festivals. email; info@poetrykit.org

Jim is widely published and all of the poems in this collection have been previously published.

Printed by JRDigital Print Services Ltd

Unit 122 John Wilson Business Park, Chestfield
Whitstable, Kent. CT5 3QY.

http://www.jrdigitalprint.co.uk/